The LANGUAGE and SENTIMENT of FLOWERS

James D. McCabe

APPLEWOOD BOOKS
Bedford, Massachusetts

CONTENTS

3

The Language and Sentiment of Flowers

The flower world is linked with all the finer sympathies of our nature. The sweet blossoms that cover the green wood are the delight of our childhood; a bouquet is the best ornament of girlish beauty: the meetest offering from young and timid love. Flowers deck the chamber of old age, and are the last sad gift of sorrow to the dead.

It was from the East that we obtained a language of perfume and beauty, which bestows a meaning on buds and blossoms, though the Turkish and Arabic flower-language does not much resemble ours. It is formed, not by an idea or sentiment originating in the flower itself, but by its capacity for rhyming with another word; i.e., the word with which the flower rhymes becomes its signification.

La Mottraie, the companion of Charles XII, brought the Eastern language of flowers to Europe; but it was the gifted Lady Mary Wortley Montague who first told the

English—speaking world how the fair maidens of the East had lent a mute speech to flowers, and could send a letter by a bouquet. She says, speaking of a Turkish love letter sent by her in a purse to a friend, "There is no color, no flower, no weed, no fruit, herb, pebble, or feather, that has not a verse belonging to it; and you may quarrel, reproach, or send letters of passion, friendship, or civility, or even of news, without even inking your fingers."

The European flower language was utilized, and almost formed, by Aim Martin; and the earlier works on the subject were only translations or adaptations from the French; but English writers have a good deal altered and modified it since; and as new flowers come yearly to us from other lands, every fresh vocabulary may contain additional words or sentences, even as our own tongue grows by grafts from other languages.

The vocabulary which is given in the following pages is believed to be complete in every respect.

JAMES D. MCCABE

The Flower-Language—
An Example

A very interesting correspondence may be maintained by means of bouquets. We give below an example of this. The message is given and then the names of the flowers needed in the bouquet to convey the message.

May maternal love protect your early youth in innocence and joy!

Flowers needed.

Moss .... *Maternal love*
Bearded Crepis .... *Protect*
Primroses .... *Early youth*
Daisy .... *Innocence*
Wood Sorrel .... *Joy*

MODIFICATIONS OF THE FLOWER-LANGUAGE

If a flower be given *reversed*, its original significance is contradicted, and the opposite meaning is implied.

A rosebud divested of its thorns, but retaining its leaves, conveys the sentiment, "I fear no longer; I hope;" thorns signifying fears, and leaves hopes.

Stripped of leaves and thorns, the bud signifies, "There is nothing to hope or fear."

The expression of flowers is also varied by changing their positions. Place a marigold on the head, and it signifies "Mental anguish;" on the bosom, "Indifference."

When a flower is given, the pronoun *I* is understood by bending it to the right hand; *thou*, by inclining it to the left.

"Yes," is implied by touching the flower given with the lips.

"No," by pinching off a petal and casting it away.

"I am," is expressed by a laurel-leaf twisted round the bouquet.

"I have," by an ivy-leaf folded together.

"I offer you," by a leaf of the Virginian creeper.

9

PART I: THE FLOWERS

Abatina
Fickleness
Abecedary
Volubility
Abutilon
Meditation
Acacia
Chaste love, Friendship
Acacia (Rose or White)
Elegance, Platonic love
Acacia (Yellow)
Secret love
Acalia
Temperance
Acanthus
Artifice
The fine arts
Achillea Millefolia
War
Achimenes Cupreata
Such worth is rare
Aconite (Crowfoot)
Luster
Aconite (Wolfsbane)
Misanthropy
Adonis (Flos)
Sad memories
Agnus Castus
Coldness, Indifference
Agrimony
Gratitude, Thankfulness
Allspice
Compassion
Almond (Common)
Indiscretion
Stupidity

Acacia—Chaste Love.

Acacia (Rose)—
Platonic Love.

Almond Tree—
Indiscretion.

Almond (Flowering)
  Hope
Almond (Laurel)
  Perfidy
Almond Tree
  Indiscretion, thoughtlessness
Aloe
  Grief, Sorrow
  Religious superstition
Althea Frutes (Syrian Mallow)
  Persuasion
Alyssum (Sweet)
  Worth beyond beauty
Amaranth
  Immortality
Amaranth (Cockscomb)
  Affection, Foppery
  Singularity
Amaranth (Globe)
  Immortality
  Unfading love
Amaryllis
  Pride
  Splendid beauty
Ambrosia
  Love returned
Amethyst
  Admiration
Andromeda
  Self-sacrifice
Anemone
  Expectation
Anemone (Garden)
  Forsaken
Anemone (Wood)
  Sickness
Anemone (Zephyr Flower)
  Expectation
  Sickness
Angelica
  Inspiration, Magic

Aloe—Sorrow.

Amaranth—Immortality.

Globe Amaranth—
Unchangeable.

Angrec
Royalty

Apocynum (Dogbane)
Deceit

Apple
Temptation

Apple Blossom
Choice, Preference

Apricot Blossom
Doubt

Arbor Vitae
Live for me
Unchanging friendship

Arbutus
Friendship, Love

Arum (Wake-Robin)
Ardor, Zeal

Arum Lily
Purity

Asclepius
Sorrowful remembrance

Ash (Mountain)
Prudence
With me you are safe

Ash Tree
Grandeur

Ash-leaved Trumpet Flower
Separation

Aspen
Fear, Lamentation

Asphodel
My regrets follow you to the grave

Aster (China)
Afterthought, Variety

Aster (Double China)
Reciprocity, I share your sentiments

Auricula
Painting
Wealth is not always happiness

Auricula (Scarlet)
Avarice

Apple Blossom—Choice.

Apricot Blossom—Doubt.

Asphodel—"My regrets follow you to the grave."

Austurtium
Splendor
Azalea
Adoration
Moderation, Temperance
True to the end
Baby's Breath
Pure of heart
Bachelor's Button
Celibacy, Single blessedness
Balm
Sympathy
Balm (Gentle)
Pleasantry
Balm of Gilead
Cure, Relief
Balmia
Nature
Balsam (Red)
Impatient resolves
Touch me not
Balsam (Yellow)
Impatience
Barberry
Sharpness of temper
Basil
Hatred
Bayberry
Discipline, Instruction
Bay Leaf
Faithfulness, I change but in death
Bay Tree
Glory
Bay Wreath
Reward of merit
Bearded Crepis
Protection
Bee Ophrys
Error
Bee Orchis
Industry

Double China-Aster—
Reciprocity.

Azalea—Adoration.

Bee Orchis—Industry.

13

Beech Tree
Prosperity
Begonia
Deformity
Bell Flower (Pyramidal)
Constancy
Bell Flower (Small white)
Gratitude
Belladonna
Silence, Hush, Death
Belvedere
I declare against you
Berry Wreath
Reward
Betony
Surprise
Bilberry
Treachery
Bindweed
Profuseness
Bindweed (Great)
Insinuation, Importunity
Bindweed (Small)
Humility
Birch Tree
Meekness
Birdsfoot Trefoil
Revenge
Bittersweet
Truth, Platonic love
Bittersweet Nightshade
Truth
Black Poplar
Courage
Black Thorn
Difficulty
Bladder Nut Tree
Amusement, Frivolity
Bluebell
Constancy
Sorrowful regret

Belladonna—Silence.

Bilberry—Treachery.

Birch Tree—Meekness.

14

Bluebottle
Constancy,
Delicacy
Bluets
Contentment
Bonus Henricus
Goodness
Borage
Bluntness
Box
Firmness
Box Tree
Stoicism
Bramble
Envy
Lowliness
Remorse
Branch of Currants
You please all
Branch of Thorns
Rigor, Severity
Broken Straws
Division
Broom
Humility
Neatness
Buckbean
Calm repose
Bugloss
Falsehood
Bulrush
Docility
Indiscretion
Bur
Rudeness, You weary me
Burdock
Importunity
Touch me not
Buttercup (Kingcup)
Childishness, Ingratitude
Desire for riches

Black Thorn—Difficulty.

Borage—Bluntness.

Broom—Humility.

Buttercups
Childhood

Butterfly Orchis
Gayety

Butterfly Weed
Let me go

Cabbage
Profit

Cacalia
Adulation

Cactus
Warmth

Calceolaria
I offer you my fortune
I offer you pecuniary assistance

Calla Lily
Magnificent beauty

Calycanthus
Benevolence

Camellia (White)
Excellence in woman
Perfected loveliness

Camellia (Red)
Pity
Unpretending excellence

Camomile
Energy in adversity

Campanula Pyramida
Aspiring

Canary Grass
Perseverance

Candytuft
Indifference

Canterbury Bell
Acknowledgment
Gratitude

Cape Jasmine
Anticipation
I am too happy

Cardamine
Paternal error

Buttercups—Childhood.

Camellia Japonica—Pity.

Camomile—
Energy in Adversity.

Cardinal Flower
Distinction
Carnation
Bonds of affection
Fascination
Pure and deep love
Carnation (Pink)
Woman's love
Carnation (Deep Red)
Alas! for my poor heart
Carnation (Striped)
Refusal, Extremes
Carnation (Yellow)
Disdain
Carrot Flower
Do not refuse me
Catalpa
Beware of the coquette
Catchfly
Snare
Catchfly (Red)
Youthful love
Catchfly (White)
Betrayed
Cattleya
Mature charms
Cedar Leaf
I live but for you
Think of me
Cedar of Lebanon
Incorruptible
Cedar Tree
Constancy, Everlasting love
Strength
Celandine (Lesser)
Joy
Joys to come
Centaury
Delicacy
Cereus (Creeping)
Modest genius

Canary Grass—
Perseverance.

Yellow Carnation—Disdain.

Celandine—Joy.

17

Cereus (Night-blooming)
Transient beauty
Champignon (Mushroom)
Suspicion
Checkered Fritillary
Persecution
Cherry blossom
Spiritual beauty
Cherry Tree
Education
Cherry Tree (White)
Deception
Chervil (Garden)
Sincerity
Chestnut Tree
Do me justice
Chickweed
Rendezvous
Chicory
Frugality
China Aster (Single)
Indecision
I will think on it
China or Indian Pink
Aversion
Chrysanthemum
Cheerfulness
Cheerfulness under adversity
Chrysanthemum (Red)
Love
Chrysanthemum (White)
Truth
Chrysanthemum (Yellow)
Slighted love
Cineraria
Always delightful
A star, Ever bright
Cinnamon
My fortune is yours
Cinnamon Tree
Forgiveness of injuries

Cherry Tree—Education.

Single China-Aster—Indecision.

Chrysanthemum—Cheerfulness.

Cinquefoil
Maternal affection
Cistus or Rock Rose
Popular favor
Citron (Lemon)
Ill-natured beauty
Clarkia
*The variety of your
conversation delights me*
Clematis
*Mental beauty
Pure love*
Clematis (Evergreen)
Poverty
Clianthus
*Self-seeking
Worldliness*
Clotbur
*Pertinacity
Rudeness*
Clover (Four-leaved)
Be mine
Clover (Red)
Industry
Clover (White)
Think of me
Clove
*I have loved you and
you have not known it*
Cloves
Dignity
Cluster Rose
"You are charming"
Cobaea
Gossip
Coltsfoot
Justice shall be done
Columbine
Folly
Columbine (Purple)
Resolution, Resolved to win

Clematis—Mental Beauty.

Cluster Rose—
"You are charming."

Purple Columbine—
Resolution.

19

Columbine (Red)
Anxious and trembling
Convolvulus
Bonds
Convolvulus (Blue, Minor)
Night, Repose
Convolvulus (Major)
Extinguished hope
Convolvulus (Pink)
*Worth sustained by judicious
and tender affection*
Corchorus
Impatient of absence
Coreopsis
Always cheerful
Coreopsis Arkansa
Love at first sight
Coriander
Hidden worth
Corn
Riches
Corn (Broken)
Quarrel
Corn Bottle
Delicacy
Corn Cockle
Gentility
Corn Flower
Purity
Corn Straw
Agreement
Corn Straw (Broken)
Disagreement, quarrel
Cornel Tree
Duration
Coronella
Success crown your wishes
Cowslip
Pensiveness, Winning grace
Cowslip (American)
*Divine beauty
You are my divinity*

Convolvulus—
Extinguished Hope.

Corn—Riches.

Corn Flower—Purity.

Coxcomb
Foppery
Crabapple Blossom
Ill-nature
Cranberry
Cure for heartache
Creeping Cereus
Horror, Modest genius
Cress
Power, Stability
Crimson Polyanthus
The heart's mystery
Crimson Poppy
Fantasy
Crocus
Abuse not
Crocus (Saffron)
Mirth
Crocus (Spring)
Youthful gladness
Crowfoot
Ingratitude
Crowfoot (Aconite-leaved)
Luster
Crown Imperial
Arrogance, Majesty, Power
Crown of Roses
Reward of chastity
Crowsbill
Envy
Cuckoo Plant
Ardor
Cucumber
Criticism
Cudweed (American)
Unceasing remembrance
Currant
Your frown will kill me
Cuscuta
Meanness
Cyclamen
Diffidence, Timid hope

Cowslip—Pensiveness.

Cranberry—
Cure for Heartache.

Crocus—Abuse not.

21

Cypress
  Death, Mourning
Cypress and Marigold
  Despair
Czar Violet
  Kindness and worth
Daffodil (Double)
  Regard
Daffodil (Great Yellow)
  Chivalry
Daffodil (Single)
  Good taste
Dahlia
  Instability
  Elegance and dignity
Dahlia (Red)
  Joy
Daisy
  Cheerfulness
  Innocence
Daisy (Double)
  Participation
Daisy (Garden)
  I share your sentiments
Daisy (Michaelmas)
  Afterthought, Farewell
Daisy (Parti-colored)
  Beauty
Daisy (Wild)
  Indecision
Dandelion
  Coquetry
  Lover's oracle, Rustic oracle
Daphne
  Gilding the Lily
  Glory, Ornament
  Immortality
Daphne Odora
  Painting the Lily
Darnel (Ray Grass)
  Vice

Czar Violet—
Kindness and Worth.

Dahlia—
Elegance and Dignity

Double Daisy—Participation.

Day Lily
  Coquetry
Deadly Nightshade
  Falsehood
Dew Plant
  A serenade
Dianthus
  Make haste
Diosma
  Your simple elegance charms me
Dittany of Crete
  Birth
Dittany of Crete (White)
  Passion
Dock
  Patience
Dodder of Thyme
  Baseness, Meanness
Dogbane
  Deceit, Falsehood
Dogwood (Flowering)
  Durability, love undiminished
Dragon Plant
  Snare
Dragonwort
  Horror
Dried Flax
  Utility
Ebony Tree
  Blackness
  "You are hard"
Eglantine (Sweetbriar)
  I wound but to heal
  Poetry
Elder
  Mercy
  Zealousness
Elm
  Dignity
Elm (American)
  Patriotism

Wild Daisy—
Indecision.

Daphne—Ornament.

Dew Plant—A Serenade.

23

Enchanters' Nightshade
Sorcery, Witchcraft
Endive
Frugality
Escholzia
Do not refuse me
Eupatorium
Delay
Everflowering Candytuft
Indifference
Evergreen Clematis
Poverty
Evergreen Thorn
Solace in adversity
Everlasting
Never-ceasing remembrance
Everlasting Pea
An appointed meeting
Lasting pleasure
Fennel
Strength
Worthy all praise
Fern
Fascination, Magic
Sincerity
Fern Moss
Content
Ficoides (Ice Plant)
Your looks freeze me
Field Red Poppy
Consolation
Fig
Argument
Fig Marigold
Idleness
Fig Tree
Prolific
Filbert Tree
Reconciliation
Fir Cone
Order

Endive—Frugality.

Fennel—Strength.

Field Red Poppy—Consolation.

Fir Tree
Elevation
First Rose of Summer
Majesty
Flax
Domestic virtues
Fate
Flax-leaved Goldenlocks
Tardiness
Fleur-de-lis
Flame, I burn
Fleur-de-Luce
Fire
Flower-of-an-Hour
Delicate beauty
Flowering Fern
Meditation, Reverie
Flowering Laurel
Goodness
Flowering Reed
Confidence in heaven
Fly Orchis
Error
Flytrap, Venus's
Deceit
Fool's Parsley
Silliness
Forget-Me-Not
True love, Undying love
Four-o'clock
Timidity
Foxglove
Insincerity
Foxtail Grass
Sporting, sport, fun
Freesia
Innocence
Fritilaria
Persecution
Frog Ophrys
Disgust

Filbert Tree—Reconciliation.

Flax—Domestic Virtues.

Flowering Fern—Meditation.

Fuchsia
Confiding love
Fuchsia (Scarlet)
Taste
Fuller's Thistle
Misanthropy
Fumitory
Spleen
Furze or Gorse
Love for all seasons
Garden Anemone
Forsaken
Garden Chervil
Sincerity
Garden Daisy
I share your sentiments
Garden Forget-me-not
"Forget me not"
Garden Marigold
Uneasiness
Garden Sage
Esteem
Gardenia
Peace
Refinement
Garland or crown of Roses
Reward of virtue
Gathered flowers
We will die together
Gentian
Intrinsic worth
Gentian (closed)
Sweet be your dreams
Gentian (fringed)
I look to heaven
Geranium
Gentility
Geranium (Black Prince)
Delusive hopes
Geranium (Dark)
Melancholy

Fuller's Thistle—
Misanthropy.

Garden Forget-me-not.
"Forget me not,"

Gardenea—Peace.

26

Geranium (Ivy)
  Bridal Favor
Geranium (Lemon)
  Unexpected meeting
Geranium (Nutmeg)
  Expected meeting
Geranium (Oak)
  Lady, deign to smile
Geranium (Oak-leaved)
  True friendship
Geranium (Pencil-leaved)
  Ingenuity, genius
Geranium (Rose/Pink)
  Preference, I prefer you
Geranium (Scarlet)
  Comfort
  Silliness, stupidity
Geranium (Silver-leaved)
  Recall, Retrospection
Geranium (Variegated)
  Charms of women
Geranium (White)
  Refinement
Geranium, Wild
  Steadfast piety
Germander Speedwell
  Facility
Gillyflower
  Bonds of affection
Gladiolus
  Ready armed
Globe Ranunculus
  "I am dazzled by your charms'
Glory Flower
  Glorious beauty
Goat's Rue
  Reason
Goldenrod
  Careful encouragement, Precaution
Gooseberry
  Anticipation

Variegated Geranium—
Charms of Women.

Globe Ranunculus—"I am dazzled by your charms."

Goat's Rue—Reason.

27

Gorse
  Enduring Affection
Gourd
  Bulk, Extent
Grape (Wild)
  Charity
  Mirth
Grass
  Humility, Submission
  Utility
Hand Flower Tree
  Warning
Harebell
  Grief
  Submission
Harlequin
  Laugh at trouble
Hawkweed
  Quick sightedness
Hawthorn
  Hope
Hazel
  Reconciliation
Heartsease (Pansy)
  Thoughts, you occupy my thoughts
  Think of me
Heath
  Solitude
Helenium
  Tears
Heliotrope
  Devotion, I turn to you
Hellebore
  Calumny
  Scandal
Helmet Flower (Monkshood)
  Knight-errantry
Hemlock
  Black magic, Evil
  You will be my death
Hemp
  Fate

Harebell—Grief.

Heliotrope—Devotion.

Hemp—Fate.

28

Henbane
Imperfection
Heps and Haws
Compensation
Hepatica
Confidence
Hibiscus
Change
Delicate beauty
Holly
Foresight
Holly (Variegated)
Always cheerful
Holly Berry
Greeting
Holly Herb
Enchantment
Hollyhock
Fecundity
Female ambition
Honesty (Lunaria)
Fascination, Honesty
Honey Flower
Love sweet and secret
Honeysuckle
Generous and devoted affection
Honeysuckle (Coral)
"The color of my fate"
Honeysuckle (French)
Rustic beauty
Honeysuckle (Monthly)
Bond of love, devoted love
Honeysuckle (Wild)
Inconstancy in love
Hop
Injustice
Hornbeam
Ornament
Horse Chestnut
Luxury
Hortensia
You are cold

Holly—Foresight.

Hollyhock—
Female Ambition.

Coral Honeysuckle—
"The colour of my fate."

29

Hothouse Leek
Exile
Houseleek
Domestic industry
Vivacity
Houstonia
Content
Hoya (Wax Plant)
Sculpture
Hoyabella
Contentment
Humble Plant
Despondency
Hundred-leaved Rose
Dignity of mind
Hyacinth
Game, Play, Sport
Hyacinth (Blue)
Constancy
Hyacinth (Purple)
Sorrow
Hyacinth (White)
Unobtrusive loveliness
Hydrangea
A boaster, Boastfulness
Heartlessness
Hyssop
Cleanliness, Purity
Ice Plant (Ficoides)
Rejected addresses
Your looks freeze me
Iceland Moss
Health
Ilex
Endurance
Imperial Montague
Power
Indian Cress
Warlike trophy
Iris
"I have a message for you," Message

Houseleek—Vivacity

Hyacinth—Sport.

Ice Plant—
Rejected Addresses.

Iris (German)
Flame, I burn
Ivy
Friendship, Fidelity
Ivy (American)
Strong friendship
Ivy (Ground)
Humility
Ivy (Irish)
Clinging affection
Ivy (Variegated)
Brightness
Ivy (White)
Rarity
Ivy Berry
Warning
Ivy Spray
Assiduous to please
Ivy Vine
Marriage
Jacob's Ladder
Come down
Jasmine
Amiability
Jasmine (Cape)
Transport of joy
Jasmine (Carolina, Virginian)
Separation
Jasmine (Indian)
I attach myself to you
Jasmine (Spanish)
Sensuality
Jasmine (White)
Amiability, Extreme amiability
Jasmine (Yellow)
Grace and elegance
Jonquil
Have pity on my passion
I desire a return of affection
Judas Tree
Betrayal, Unbelief

Iris—"I have a message for you."

Ivy—Friendship.

White Jasmine—
Extreme Amiability.

31

Juniper
  Protection, Succor
Justicia
  The perfection of female loveliness
Kennedia
  Mental beauty
Kingcup
  Desire of riches
  "I wish I was rich"
Laburnum
  Forsaken
  Pensive beauty
Lady's Slipper
  Capricious beauty
  Win me and wear me
Lady's Smock
  Ardor
Lady's Thimble
  Grief
  Submission
Lady's Tresses
  Bewitching grace
Lagerstraemia (Indian)
  Eloquence
Lantana
  Rigor, I am unyielding
Larch
  Audacity, Boldness
Larch Fir
  Deceitful charms
Larkspur
  Brightness
  Lightness, Levity
Larkspur (Pink)
  Fickleness
Larkspur (Purple)
  Haughtiness
Laurel (Mountain)
  Ambition, Glory
Laurel (Common, in flower)
  Perfidy, Treachery

Juniper—Protection.

Kingcup—
"I wish I was rich."

Laburnum—Forsaken.

Laurel (Ground)
  Perseverance
Laurel (Variegated)
  Attractive
Laurel-leaved Magnolia
  Dignity
Laurustinus
  "I die if neglected"
Lavatera
  Sweet disposition
Lavender
  Distrust
  Failure
Lemon
  Ill-natured beauty
  Piquancy, Zest
Lemon Blossoms
  Discretion
  Fidelity in love
Leschenaultia Splendens
  You are charming
Lettuce
  Cold-heartedness
Lichen
  Dejection
  Solitude
Licorice (Wild)
  I declare against you
Lignum Vitae
  Homage
Lilac (Field)
  Humility
Lilac (Purple)
  First emotions of love
Lilac (White)
  Purity and modesty
  Youthful innocence
Lily
  Modesty, Purity
Lily (Day)
  Coquetry

Laurel—Ambition.

Laurustinus—
"I die if neglected."

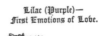

Lilac (Purple)—
First Emotions of Love.

33

Lily (Imperial)
Dignity, Majesty
Lily (Lenten)
Reciprocal love
Lily (Water)
Eloquence
Lily (White)
Purity, Sweetness
Lily (Yellow)
Falsehood, Lies
Lily of the Valley
Return of happiness
Linden or Lime Tree
Conjugal love
Linden (American)
Matrimony
Lint
Obligation, I feel my obligations
Live Oak
Liberty
Liverwort
Confidence
Lobelia
Malevolence
Locust Tree
Elegance
Locust Tree (Green)
Affection beyond the grave
London Pride
Frivolity
Lote Tree
Concord
Lotus
Eloquence
Lotus Flower
Estranged love
Lotus Leaf
Recantation
Love-in-Idleness
Love at first sight
Love-in-a-Mist
Perplexity

Lily of the Valley—
Return of Happiness.

Lotus Flower—
Estranged Love.

Love-lies-Bleeding—
Hopeless.

Love-Lies-Bleeding
Hopeless, not heartless
Lucerne
Life
Lupine
Imagination
Voraciousness
Lupine (White)
Always happy
Lupine (Rose)
Fanciful
Madder
Calumny
Madwort
Happiness, Tranquility
Magnolia
Love of nature
Magnolia (Laurel-leaved)
Dignity
Magnolia (Swamp)
Perseverance
Maidenhair Fern
Secrecy
Mallow
Mildness
Mallow (Marsh)
Kindness
Beneficience
Mallow (Syrian)
Consumed by love
Mallow (Venetian)
Delicate beauty
Manchineal Tree
Falsehood
Mandrake
Horror
Maple
Reserve
Marianthus
Hope for better days
Marigold
Grief, pain, trouble

Magnolia—Love of Nature.

Maiden-hair Fern—Secrecy.

Marshmallow—
Kindness.

35

Marigold (African)
Vulgar minds
Marigold (French)
Jealousy
Marigold (Prophetic)
Prediction
Marigold and Cypress
Despair
Marjoram
Blushes
Marvel of Peru
Timidity
Mayflower
Welcome
Meadow Lychnis
Wit
Meadow Saffron
My best days are past
Meadowsweet
Uselessness
Mercury
Goodness
Mezereon
Desire to please
Mignonette
Excellence
Your qualities surpass your charms
Milfoil (Achillea Millefolia)
War
Milkvetch
Your presence softens my pains
Milkwort
Hermitage
Mimosa (Sensitive Plant)
Sensitiveness
Mint
Virtue
Mistletoe
I surmount all obstacles
Mock Orange
Counterfeit

Marjoram—Blushes.

Mignonette—Excellence.

Mint—Virtue.

Monkshead
A deadly foe is near
Monkshood (Helmet Flower)
Chivalry
Knight-errantry
Moon Daisy
Love's oracle
Moonflower
I only dream of love
Moonwort
Forgetfulness
Morning Glory
Affectation, coquetry
Moschatel
Weakness
Moss
Maternal love
Moss Rosebud
Confession of love
Mosses
Ennui, Seclusion
Mossy Saxifrage
Affection
Motherwort
Concealed love
Mountain Ash
Intellect, Prudence
With me you are safe
Mourning Bride
I have lost all
Unfortunate attachment
Mouse-eared Chickweed
Ingenuous simplicity
Mouse-eared Scorpion Grass
Forget me not
Mudwort
Tranquility
Mugwort
Happiness
Mulberry Tree (Black)
I shall not survive you

Moon Daisy—
Love's Oracle.

Rosebud (Moss)—
Confession of Love.

Moss—Seclusion.

37

Mulberry Tree (White)
Wisdom
Mullein
Take courage
Mullein (White)
Good nature
Mushroom (Champignon)
Mistrust, Suspicion
Musk Plant
Weakness
Mustard
I am hurt
Mustard Seed
Indifference
Myrobalan
Privation
Myrrh
Gladness
Myrtle
Love, Love in absence
Myrtle (Wax)
Discipline, Instruction
Narcissus
Egotism, Excessive self-love
Nasturtium
Patriotism
Nettle (Burning)
Slander
Nettle (Common Stinging)
You are spiteful
Nettle Tree
Conceit
Nightshade
Falsehood
Nut Tree
Amusement
Oak Leaf
Bravery, Valor
Oak Tree
Hospitality
Oak (White)
Independence

Mustard—Indifference.

Myrrh—Gladness.

Myrtle—Love.

Oats
The witching soul of music
Oleander
Beware
Olive
Peace
Orange Blossom
Chastity
Your purity equals your loveliness
Orange Tree
Generosity
Orchis
A beauty, A belle
Osier
Frankness
Osmunda
Dreams
Ox Eye
Patience
Palm
Victory
Pansy (Heartsease)
Thoughts, Think of me
You occupy my thoughts
Parsley
Feasting, Festivity
Pasque Flower
You have no claims
Passion Flower
Belief, Religious fervor
Pea (Everlasting)
Appointed meeting
Lasting pleasure
Pea (Sweet)
Departure
Peach
Your qualities, like your
charms, are unequalled
Peach Blossom
"I am your captive"
Pear
Affection

Narcissus—Egotism.

Orange Blossom—Chastity.

Everlasting Pea—
"Wilt thou go with me?"

39

Pear Tree
Affection
Comfort
Pennyroyal
Flee away
Peony
Anger
Bashfulness, Shame
Peppermint
Cordiality, Warmth of feeling
Periwinkle
Sweet memories
Periwinkle (Blue)
Early friendship
Periwinkle (White)
Pleasant recollections
Persicaria
Restoration
Persimmon
Bury me amid nature's beauties
Petunia
Your presence soothes me
Pheasant's Eye
I can't forget you, Remembrance
Phlox
Unanimity
Phlox (Star-shaped)
Affability
Pigeon Berry
Indifference
Pimpernel
Assignation, Change
Pine
Endurance
Pity
Pine (Pitch)
Philosophy
Pine (Spruce)
Farewell
Hope in adversity
Pineapple
Perfection, You are perfect

Peony—Anger.

Peppermint—Cordiality.

Pink—Boldness.

Pink
  Boldness
Pink (Double Red)
  Pure and ardent love
Pink (Indian Double)
  Always lovely
Pink (Mountain)
  Ambition, Aspirations
Pink (Single)
  Pure love
Pink (Variegated)
  Refusal
Pink (White)
  Ingeniousness, Talent
Plane Tree
  Genius
Plantain (White)
  Man's footsteps
Plum (Indian)
  Privation, Suffering
Plum Blossom
  Fidelity
Plum (Wild)
  Indepencence
Polyanthus
  Pride of riches
Polyanthus (Crimson)
  The heart's mystery
Polyanthus (Lilac)
  Confidence in heaven
Pomegranate
  Folly, Foolishness
Pomegranate Blossom
  A warning
Pomegranate Flower
  Mature elegance
  Perfection
Poor Robin
  Compensation
  Of an equivalent
Poplar (Black)
  Courage

Crimson Polyanthus—
The Heart's Mystery.

Lilac Polyanthus—
Confidence in Heaven.

Pomegranate Blossom—
A Warning.

41

Poplar (White)
Time
Poppy (Red)
Consolation
Poppy (Scarlet)
Fantastic extravagance
Poppy (Variegated)
Dreaminess, Flirtation
Poppy (White)
Forgetfulness, Oblivion, Sleep
Potato
Benevolence
Prickly Pear
Satire
Pride of China
Dissension
Primrose
Early youth
Primrose (Chinese)
Lasting love
Primrose (Evening)
Inconstancy
Primrose (Red)
Unpatronized merit
Primula
Animation
Privet
Prohibition
Pyrus Japonica
Love at first sight
Faeries' Fire
Pyxie
Life is sweet
Quaking Grass
Agitation
Quamoclit
Busybody
Queen of the Meadows
Uselessness
Queen's Rocket
Fashion
You are the queen of coquettes

Pyrus Japonica—
Love at First Sight.

Primrose—Youth.

Primula—Animation.

Quince
Temptation
Ragged-robin
Wit
Ranunculus
You are radiant with charms
Ranunculus (Garden)
You are rich in attractions
Ranunculus (Wild)
Inconstancy, Ingratitude
Raspberry
Remorse
Ray Grass (Darnel)
Vice
Reeds (With their panicles)
Music
Reed
Complaisance
Music
Reed (Split)
Indiscretion
Rhododendron (Rosebay)
Beware, Danger
Rhubarb
Advice
Rocket
Rivalry
Rose
Love
Rose (Austrian)
You are all that is lovely
Rose (Bridal)
Happy love
Rose (Burgundy)
Unconscious beauty
Unconsciousness
Rose (Cabbage)
Ambassador of love
Rose (Campion)
Only deserve my love
Rose (Carolina)
Love is dangerous

Garden Ranunculus—
"You are rich in attraction."

Wild Ranunculus—
Inconstancy.

Rose (Bridal)—Happy Love.

43

Rose (China)
Beauty always new
Grace
Rose (Christmas)
Relieve my anxiety
Tranquilize my anxiety
Rose (Daily)
Welcome me
Rose (Damask)
Freshness, Brilliant complexion
Rose (Deep Red)
Bashfulness, Bashful shame
Rose (Dog)
Pleasure and pain
Rose (Dundee Rambler)
Only deserve my love
Rose (Full-blown placed over two buds)
Secrecy
Rose (Gloire de Dijon)
Gladness
Rose (Guelder)
Growing old, Old age, Winter
Rose (Half-blown)
Timid love
Rose (Hundred-leaved)
Pride
Rose (Japan)
Compassion
Beauty is your only attraction
Rose (Lancaster)
Union
Rose (Maiden Blush)
"If you love me you will find it out"
Timid love
Rose (Monthly)
Beauty every new
Rose (Moss)
Superior merit
Rose (Multiflora)
Grace

44

Rose (Gloire de Dijon)—
Gladness.

Rose (Japan) —Compassion

Rose (White)—
"I am worthy of you."

Rose (Mundi)
  Variety
Rose (Musk)
  A capricious beauty
Rose (Pink)
  Secret love
Rose (Red–leaved)
  Beauty
Rose (Santenay)
  Pride
Rose (Single)
  Simplicity
Rose (Thornless)
  Early attachment
Rose (Unique)
  "Call me not beautiful"
  Modesty
Rose (White)
  "I am worthy of you"
Rose (White, dried)
  Death preferable to loss
  of innocence
Rose (White withered)
  Transient impressions
Rose (White and Red together)
  Unity
Rose (Wild)
  Charming simplicity
Rose (Yellow)
  Departure of love, Jealousy
Rose (York)
  War
Rosebud (Monthly)
  Enchantment
Rosebud (Red)
  Pure and lovely, Youthful
  You are young and beautiful
Rosebud (White)
  Girlhood, Innocence
  A heart ignorant of love
Rose cluster (Musk)
  Charming

Rose (White and Red)—
Unity.

Rose (Yellow)—
Departure of Love.

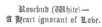

Rosebud (White)—
A Heart ignorant of Love.

45

Rosemary
Remembrance

Rudbeckia
Impartiality, Justice

Rue
Disdain

Rush, Bulrush
Docility

Rye Grass
Changeable disposition

Saffron
Beware of excess
Marriage, Voluptuousness

Saffron (Meadow)
My happiest days are past

Sage
Domestic virtues

Sage (Garden)
Esteem

Sainfoin
Agitation

Saint John's Wort
Animosity
Superstition

Salvia (Blue)
Wisdom

Salvia (Red)
Energy, Pomp

Sardony
Irony

Satin Flower
Am I forgotten?

Saxifrage (Mossy)
Affection

Scabious
Unfortunate love

Scabious (Sweet)
Widowhood

Scarlet Lychnis
Sunbeaming eyes

46

Schinus
Religious enthusiasm

Sage—Domestic Virtues.

Shamrock—Joy in Sorrow.

Red Salvia—Pomp.

Scotch Fir
Elevation
Sensitive Plant
Delicate feelings, Sensitiveness
Senvy
Indifference
Service Tree
Prudence
Shamrock
Joy in sorrow
Light-heartedness
Loyalty
Shepherd's Purse
I offer you my all
Snakesfoot
Horror
Snapdragon
Presumption
Snowball (var. Snow Berry)
Bound
Thoughts of heaven
Snowdrop
Hope
Sorrel
Parental affection
Sorrel (Wild)
Ill-timed wit
Sorrel (Wood)
Joy
Maternal tenderness
Southernwood
Jest, Merriment, Banter
Spearmint
Warmth of sentiment
Speedwell
Female fidelity
Speedwell (Germander)
Facility
Speedwell (Spiked)
Semblance
Spider Ophrys
Adroitness

Snowdrop—Hope.

Sorrel—Parental Affection.

Southernwood—Merriment.

47

Spiderwort
Esteem, not love
Spiked Willow Herb
Pretension
Spindle Tree
*Your charms are engraven
on my heart*
Star of Bethlehem
*Purity
Reconciliation*
Starwort
Afterthought
Starwort (American)
*Cheerfulness in old age
Welcome to a stranger*
Stock
Lasting beauty
Stock (Night-scented)
Devotion
Stock (Ten Week)
Promptitude, Promptness
Stonecrop
Tranquility
Straw (Broken)
*Division
Rupture of a contract*
Straw (Whole)
Agreement, Union
Strawberry
Perfect excellence
Strawberry Blossoms
Foresight
Strawberry Tree (Arbutus)
Esteem and love
Sultan Lilac
I forgive you
Sultan (Sweet)
Felicity, Happiness
Sultan (White)
Sweetness
Sultan (Yellow)
Contempt

Stock—Promptitude.

Stonecrop—Tranquillity.

Sunflower—Adoration.

Sumach (Venice)
  Intellectual excellence
  Splendor
Sunflower (Dwarf)
  Adoration
Sunflower (Tall)
  Haughtiness
Swallow-wort
  Cure for heartache
Sweet Basil
  Good wishes
Sweet Pea
  Departure
  Delicate pleasures
Sweet Sultan
  Felicity
Sweet William
  Gallantry
Sweetbriar (American)
  Simplicity
Sweetbriar (European)
  I wound but to heal
Sweetbriar (Yellow)
  Decrease of love
Sycamore
  Curiosity
Syringa
  Memory
Syringa (Carolina)
  Disappointment
Tamarisk
  Crime
Tansy (Wild)
  I declare war against you
Tendrils of Climbing Plants
  Links, Ties
Thistle (Common)
  Austerity
Thistle (Fuller's)
  Misanthropy
Thistle (Scotch)
  Retaliation

Sweet Pea—Departure.

Tendrils of Climbing Plants—Links.

Scotch Thistle—Retaliation.

49

Thorn Apple
Deceitful charms

Thorn (Branch of), Thorns
Severity

Thrift
Sympathy

Throatwort
Neglected beauty

Thyme
Activity or courage
Thriftiness

Tiger Flower
For once may pride
befriend me

Traveller's Joy
Safety

Tree of Life
Old age

Trefoil
Revenge, Vengeance

Tremella Nestoc
Resistance

Trillium Pictum
Modest beauty

Truffle
Surprise

Trumpet Flower
Fame

Tuberose
Dangerous pleasures

Tulip
Fame

Tulip (Red)
Confession of love
Declaration of love

Tulip (Variegated)
Beautiful eyes

Tulip (Yellow)
Hopeless love

Tulip Tree
Fame

Traveller's Joy—Safety.

Red Tulip—
Confession of Love.

Valerian—
Accommodating Disposition.

Turnip blossom
Charity
Tussilage (Sweet-scented)
Justice shall be done you
Valerian
An accommodating disposition
Valerian (Greek blue-flowered)
Rupture
Valerian (Red)
Readiness
Venus Car
Fly with me
Venus's Flytrap
Deceit, Duplicity
Venus's Looking-glass
Flattery

Venus's Looking-glass—
Flattery.

Verbena
Enchantment
Verbena (Pink)
Family union
Verbena (Scarlet)
Unite against evil
Church unity
Verbena (Purple)
Regret
Verbena (White)
Pray for me
Vernal Grass
Poor but happy
Veronica
Fidelity
Veronica Speciosa
Keep this for my sake
Vervain
Enchantment
Vetch
I cling to thee
Vine
Intoxication
Violet (Blue)
Faithfulness

Verbena—Enchantment.

Blue Violet—
Faithfulness.

51

Violet (Dame)
Watchfulness
Violet (Purple)
"You occupy my thoughts"
Violet (Sweet)
Modesty
Violet (White)
Innocence, Modesty, Purity
Violet (Wild)
Love in idleness
Violet (Yellow)
Rural Happiness
Virginian Creeper
Sweet neglect
I cling to you in both sunshine and shade
Virginian Spiderwort
Momentary happiness
Virgin's Bower
Filial love
Volkamenia
May you be happy!
Wake-Robin
Ardor, Zeal
Wallflower
Fidelity in adversity
Walnut Tree
Intellect, Stratagem
Walnuts
Sociality
Watcher by the Wayside
Never despair
Water Lily
Invocation
Purity of heart
Water Melon
Bulkiness
Wax Plant
Susceptibility
Wheat Stalk
Prosperity, Riches

Purple Violet—
"You occupy my thoughts."

Virginian Creeper—
Sweet Neglect.

Wallflower—Fidelity.

Whin
Anger
Whortleberry
Treason
Willow (Common)
Forsaken
Willow (Creeping)
Love forsaken
Willow (French)
Bravery and humanity
Willow (Water)
Freedom
Willow (Weeping)
Melancholy, Mourning
Willow Herb
Pretension
Winter Cherry
Deception
Wisteria
Regret
Welcome fair stranger
Witch Hazel
A spell
Mysticism
Withered Leaves
Melancholy, Sadness
Woodbine
Fraternal love
Wormwood
Absence
Xanthium
Pertinacity
Rudeness
Yarrow
Cure for heartache
Yew
Sadness, Sorrow
Zephyr Flower (Anemone)
Expectation
Zinnia
Thoughts of absent friends

Water-Lily—Invocation.

Wood Sorrel—Joy.

Yew—Sadness.

53

PART II: THE MEANINGS

Absence
  Wormwood

Abuse not
  Crocus

Accommodating disposition
  Valerian

Acknowledgment
  Canterbury Bell

Activity or courage
  Thyme

Admiration
  Amethyst

Adoration
  Azalea
  Dwarf Sunflower

Adroitness
  Spider Ophrys

Adulation
  Cacalia

Advice
  Rhubarb

Affectation
  Amaranth (Cockscomb)
  Morning Glory

Affection
  Mossy Saxifrage
  Pear Tree, Pear
  Sorrel

Affection beyond the grave
  Locust Tree (Green)

Afterthought
  Michaelmas Daisy
  China Aster
  Starwort

Agitation
  Moving Plant
  Quaking-grass
  Sainfoin

Wormwood — Absence.

Pear Tree — Affection.

Michaelmas Daisy — Afterthought.

Agreement
  Corn Straw
A Heart Ignorant of Love
  White Rosebud
Alas! for my poor heart
  Deep Red Carnation
Always cheerful
  Coreopsis
  Variegated Holly
Always delightful
  Cineraria
Always lovely
  Indian Double Pink
Am I forgotten?
  Satin Flower (Godetia)
Ambassador of love
  Cabbage Rose
Ambition
  Mountain Laurel, Mountain Pink
Ambition (Female)
  Hollyhock
Amiability (Extreme)
  White Jasmine
Amusement
  Nut Tree
Anger
  Peony
  Whin
Animation
  Primula
Animosity
  Saint John's Wort
Anticipation
  Cape Jasmine
  Gooseberry
Anxious and trembling
  Red Columbine
Appointed meeting,
Lasting pleasure
  Everlasting Pea

Variegated Holly—
Always Cheerful.

Indian Double Pink—
Always Lovely.

Rose (Cabbage)—
Ambassador.

55

Ardent love
Red Double Pink
Ardor
Arum Lily
Cuckoo Plant
Ardor, Zeal
Arum (Wake Robin)
Argument
Fig
Aspiring
Campanula Pyramida
Aspirings, Ambition
Mountain Pink
Assiduous to please
Ivy Sprig with tendrils
Assignation
Pimpernel
Attachment
Indian Jasmine (Ipomoea)
Attractive
Variegated Laurel
Audacity, Boldness
Larch
Austerity
Common Thistle
Avarice
Scarlet Auricula
Aversion
China or Indian Pink
Bantering, jest, merriment
Southernwood
Baseness
Dodder of Thyme
Bashfulness, Bashful shame
Deep Red Rose
Bashfulness
Peony
Be mine
Four-leaved Clover
Be prudent
Triptilion Spinosum

Arum Lily—Ardour.

Thistle—Austerity.

Rose (Deep Red)—
Bashfulness.

Be warned in time
Echites Atropurporea
Beautiful eyes
Variegated Tulip
A Beauty, A Belle
Orchis
Beauty
Parti-colored Daisy
Red-leaved Rose
Beauty always new
China Rose
Beauty is your only attraction
Japan Rose
Belief, Religious Fervor
Passion Flower
Beneficence
Marsh Mallow
Benevolence
Calycanthus
Potato
Betrayal, Unbelief
Judas Tree
Betrayed
White Catchfly
Beware
Oleander
Rhododendron
Beware of excess
Saffron
Beware of false friends
Franciscea Latifolia
Birth
Dittany of Crete
Blackness
Ebony Tree
Bluntness
Borage
Blushes
Marjoram
Boastfulness
Hydrangea

Orchis—A Beauty.

Parti-coloured Daisy—
Beauty.

Hydrangea—Boastfulness.

57

Boldness
  Pink
  Larch
Bond of Love
  Monthly Honeysuckle
Bonds
  Convolvulus
Bonds of affection
  Gillyflower
Bound
  Snowball
Bravery, Valor
  Oak Leaf
Bravery and humanity
  French Willow
Bridal favor
  Ivy Geranium
Bridal festivities
  Orange Flowers
Brightness
  Variegated Ivy
Brilliant complexion, Freshness
  Damask Rose
Bulk, Extent
  Gourd
Bulkiness
  Water Melon
Bury me amid nature's beauties
  Persimmon
Busybody
  Quamoclit
Call me not beautiful
  Unique Rose
Calm repose
  Buckbean
Calumny
  Hellebore
  Madder
Candor, Frankness
  Osier

Monthly Honeysuckle—
Bond of Love.

Variegated Ivy--Brightness.

Rose (Musk)—
A Capricious Beauty.

58

Capricious beauty
  Musk Rose
  Lady's Slipper
Celibacy
  Bachelor's Button
Change
  Hibiscus
  Pimpernel
Changeable disposition
  Rye Grass
Charity
  Turnip Blossom
  Wild Grape
Charming
  Musk Rose Cluster
Charms of women
  Variegated Geranium
Chaste love, Friendship
  Acacia
Chastity
  Orange Blossom
Cheerfulness
  Daisy
Cheerfulness in old age
  American Starwort
Cheerfulness under adversity, Cheerfulness
  Chrysanthemum
Childishness, Ingratitude
  Buttercup
Chivalry
  Daffodil
Chivalry, Knight-errantry
  Monkshood (Helmet Flower)
Cleanliness
  Hyssop
Clinging affection
  Irish Ivy
Cold heartedness
  Lettuce
Coldness, Indifference
  Aguas Castus

Hibiscus—Change.

Daffodil—Chivalry.

Irish Ivy—
Clinging Affection.

"Color of my fate, The"
  Coral Honeysuckle
Come down.
  Jacob's Ladder
Comfort
  Pear Tree
  Scarlet Geranium
Compassion
  Allspice
  Japan Rose
Compensation
  Heps and Haws
Compensation,
  Poor Robin
Complaisance,
  Reed
Concealed love
  Motherwort
Conceit
  Nettle Tree
Concord
  Lote Tree
Confession of love
  Moss Rosebud
  Red Tulip
Confidence
  Hepatica
  Liverwort
Confidence in heaven
  Flowering Reed
  Lilac Polyanthus
Conjugal love
  Linden, Lime Tree
Consolation
  Red Poppy
Constancy
  Blue Hyacinth
  Pyramidal Bell Flower
Constancy, Delicacy
  Bluebottle

Heps and Haws—
Compensation.

Hepatica—Confidence.

Linden—Conjugal Love.

60

Constancy, Everlasting love
  Cedar Tree
Constancy, Sorrowful regret
  Bluebell
Consumed by love
  Syrian Mallow
Contempt
  Yellow Sultan
Content
  Fern Moss
  Houstonia
Contentment
  Hoyabella
Coquetry
  Day Lily
Cordiality
  Peppermint
Could you bear poverty?
  Browallia Jamisonii
Counterfeit
  Mock Orange
Courage
  Black Poplar
Crime
  Tamarisk
Criticism
  Cucumber
Cure for heartache
  Cranberry
  Swallow-wort
Cure, Relief
  Balm of Gilead
Curiosity
  Sycamore
Danger, Beware
  Rhododendron (Rosebay)
Dangerous pleasures
  Tuberose
Dark melancholy
  Geranium

Bluebell—Constancy.

Day Lily—Coquetry.

Rhododendron—Danger.

61

"Deadly foe is near, A"
  Monkshood
Death preferable to
loss of innocence
  White Rose (Dried)
Death, Mourning
  Cypress
Deceit
  Venus's Flytrap
Deceit, Falsehood
  Dogbane (Apocynum)
Deceitful charms
  Larch Fir
  Thorn Apple
Deception
  White Cherry Tree
  Winter Cherry
Declaration of love
  Red Tulip
Decrease of love
  Yellow Rose
  Yellow Sweetbriar
Deformity
  Begonia
Dejection, Solitude
  Lichen
Delay
  Eupatorium
Delicacy
  Centaury
  Corn Bottle
Delicate beauty
  Flower-of-an-Hour
  Hibiscus
  Venetian Mallow
Delicate pleasures
  Sweet Pea
Delusive hopes
  Black Prince Geranium
Departure
  Sweet Pea

White Cherry Tree—
Deception.

Red Tulip—
Declaration of Love.

Black Prince Geranium—
Delusive Hopes.

Departure of love, Jealousy
  Yellow Rose
Desire of riches
  Kingcup
Desire to please
  Mezereon
Despair
  Cypress
  Marigold
Despondency
  Humble Plant
Devotion
  Night-scented Stock
  Peruvian Heliotrope
Devotion or I turn to thee
  Heliotrope
Difficulty
  Black Thorn
Diffidence
  Cyclamen
Dignity
  Cloves
  Elm
  Laurel-leaved Magnolia
Dignity, Majesty
  Imperial Lily
Dignity of mind
  Hundred-leaved Rose
Disappointment
  Carolina Syringa
Disdain
  Yellow Carnation
  Rue
Disgust
  Frog Ophrys
Dissension
  Pride of China
Distinction
  Cardinal Flower
Distrust
  Lavender

Rose (Yellow)—
Departure of Love.

Heliotrope—Devotion.

Imperial Lily—Dignity.

63

Divine beauty
American Cowslip
Division
Broken Straw
Do me justice
Chestnut Tree
Docility,
Indiscretion
Bullrush, Rush
Domestic industry
Houseleek
Domestic virtues, Fate
Flax
Sage
Doubt
Apricot Blossom
Dreams
Osmunda
Durability
Dogwood
Duration
Cornel Tree
Early attachments
Thornless Rose
Early friendships
Red Periwinkle
Early youth and sadness
Primrose
Education
Cherry Tree
Egotism, Excessive self-love
Narcissus
Elegance
Locust Tree
Elegance and Dignity
Dahlia
Elegance, Platonic love
Rose or White Acacia
Elevation
Fir Tree
Scotch Fir

Bullrush—Docility.

Osmunda—Dreams.

Red Periwinkle—
Early Friendships.

Eloquence
  Lotus
Enchantment
  Holly Herb
  Monthly Rose-bud
  Verbena
  Vervain
Endurance
  Ilex
Enduring affection
  Gorse
Energy
  Red Salvia
Energy in adversity
  Camomile
Ennui
  Mosses
Envy
  Bramble
  Crowsbill
Error
  Bee Ophrys
  Fly Orchis
Esteem
  Garden Sage
Esteem not love
  Spiderwort
Esteem and love
  Strawberry Tree
Estranged love
  Lotus Flower
Excellence
  Mignonette
Excellence in woman
  White Camellia
Exile
  Hothouse Heath
Expectation
  Zephyr Flower (Anemone)
Expected meeting
  Nutmeg Geranium

Gorse—
Enduring Affection.

White Camellia—
Excellence in Woman.

Nutmeg Geranium—
An Expected Meeting.

65

Extent, Bulk
  Gourd
Extinguished hopes
  Convolvulus Major
Extreme Amiability
  White Jasmine
Extremes, Refusal
  Striped Carnation
Facility
  Germander Speedwell
Fairies' fire
  Pyrus Japonica
Faithfulness
  Blue Violet
Falsehood
  Bugles
  Deadly Nightshade
  Dogbane
  Manchineal Tree
Falsehood, Gayety and lies
  Yellow Lily
Fame
  Trumpet Flower
  Tulip Tree
Family Union
  Pink Verbena
Fantastic extravagance
  Scarlet Poppy
Fantasy
  Crimson Poppy
Farewell,
  Spruce Pine
Farewell or afterthought
  Michaelmas Daisy
Fascination
  Honesty (Lunaria)
Fascination, Magic,
  Fern
Fashion
  Queen's Rocket

Striped Carnation—
Extremes.

Yellow Lily—Falsehood.

Crimson Poppy—Fantasy.

Fate
  Flax
  Hemp
Fear
  Aspen
Feasting, Festivity
  Parsley
Felicity
  Sweet Sultan
Female ambition,
Fecundity
  Hollyhock
Female fidelity
  Speedwell
Fickleness
  Abatina
  Pink Larkspur
Fidelity
  Plum Tree
  Veronica
Fidelity in adversity
  Wallflower
Fidelity in love
  Lemon Blossoms
Filial love
  Virgin's Bower
Fine arts, Artifice
  Acanthus
Fire
  Fleur-de-Luce
Firmness
  Box
First emotions of love
  Purple Lilac
Flame
  German Iris
Flame, I burn
  Fleur-de-lis
Flattery
  Venus's Looking-glass

Parsley—Feasting.

Pink Larkspur—Fickleness.

Acanthus—The Fine Arts.

67

Flee away
Pennyroyal
Fly with me
Venus Car
Folly, Foolishness
Columbine
Pomegranate
Foppery, Affectation, Singularity
Cockscomb Amaranth
For once may pride befriend me
Tiger Flower
Foresight
Holly
Strawberry Blossoms
Forget me not
Garden Forget-me-not
Mouse-eared Scorpion Grass
Forgetfulness
Moonwort
Forsaken
Garden Anemone
Laburnum
Willow
Frankness, Candor
Osier
Fraternal love
Woodbine
Freedom
Water Willow
Freshness, Brilliant complexion
Damask Rose
Friendship, Chaste love
Acacia
Friendship, Fidelity, Marriage
Ivy
Frivolity, Amusement
Bladder Nut Tree
London Pride
"Frown will kill me, Thy"
Currant

Pomegranate—Folly.

Garden Anemone—
Forsaken.

Rose (Damask)—Freshness.

Frugality
  Chicory
  Endive
Gallantry
  Sweet William
Game, Play, Sport
  Hyacinth
Gayety
  Butterfly Orchis
Gayety and lies
  Yellow Lily
Generosity
  Orange Tree
Generous and devoted affection
  Honeysuckle
Genius
  Pencil-leaved Geranium
  Plane Tree
Gentility
  Corn Cockle
Gentle Pleasantry
  Balm
Girlhood, A heart ignorant of love
  White Rosebud
Girlhood, Youthful beauty
  Red Rosebud
Gladness
  Dijon Rose
  Myrrh
Glorious beauty
  Glory Flower
Glory
  Bay Tree
  Laurel
Glory, Immortality
  Daphne
Good nature
  White Mullein
Good wishes
  Sweet Basil

Iby—Friendship.

Orange—Generosity.

Rosebud (Red) – "You are young and beautiful."

69

Goodness
  Bonus Henricus
  Flowering Laurel
  Mercury
Gossip
  Cobrea
Grace
  Rose Multiflora
Grace, Beauty always new
  China Rose
Grace and elegance
  Yellow Jasmine
Grandeur
  Ash Tree
Gratitude
  Agrimony
  Bell Flower (small white)
Great insinuation, Importunity
  Bindweed
Greeting
  Holly Berry
Grief
  Harebell
  Lady's Thimble
  Marigold
Grief, Sorrow
  Aloe
Growing old
  Guelder Rose
Happiness, Tranquility
  Madwort
Happy love
  Bridal Rose
Hatred
  Basil
Haughtiness
  Purple Larkspur
  Tall Sunflower
Health
  Iceland Moss

Rose (China)—Grace.

Ash Tree—Grandeur.

Holly Berry—Greeting.

70

Heart ignorant of love, A
White Rosebud
"Heart's mystery, The"
Crimson Polyanthus
Hermitage
Milkwort
Hidden worth
Coriander
Homage
Lignum Vitae
Honesty,
Fascination
Honesty (Lunaria)
Hope
Cyclamen
Flowering Almond
Hawthorn
Snowdrop
Hope for better days
Marianthus
Hope in adversity,
Spruce Pine
Hopeless love
Yellow Tulip
Hopeless, not heartless
Love Lies Bleeding
Horror
Creeping Cereus
Dragonwort
Mandrake
Snakesfoot
Hospitality
Oak Tree
Humility
Field Lilac
Ground Ivy
Small Bindweed
Humility,
Neatness
Broom

Honesty—Fascination.

Cyclamen—Hope.

Hawthorn—Hope.

71

I am dazzled by your charms
Globe Ranunculus

I am too happy
Cape Jasmine

I am worthy of you
White Rose

I am your captive
Peach Blossom

I attach myself to you
Indian Jasmine

I burn
Fleur-de-lis

I change but in death
Bay Leaf

I claim at least your esteem
Potentilla

I cling to you in both
sunshine and shade
Virginian Creeper

I declare against you
Belvedere
Wild Licorice

I declare war against you
Wild Tansy

I desire a return of affection
Jonquil

I die if neglected
Laurustinus

I feel my obligations
Lint

I forgive you
Sultan Lilac

I have lost all
Mourning Bride

I live for thee
Cedar Leaf

I offer you my all
Shepherd's Purse

I offer you my fortune,
I offer you pecuniary assistance
Calceolaria

Rose (White)—
"I am worthy of you."

Peach Blossom—
"I am your captive."

Cedar Leaf—
"I live for thee."

I partake your sentiments
  Double China Aster
I shall die tomorrow
  Cistus Guru
I shall not survive you
  Black Mulberry Tree
I share your sentiments
  Garden Daisy
I surmount all obstacles
  Mistletoe
I turn to you
  Heliotrope
I will think on it, Indecision
  Single China Aster
  Wild Daisy
I wish I was rich
  Kingcup
I wound but to heal
  European Sweetbriar
Idleness
  Fig Marigold
If you love me you will find it out
  Maiden Blush Rose
Ignorance of love
  Bud of White Rose
Ill-nature
  Crab Blossom
Ill-natured beauty
  Lemon (Citron)
Immortality
  Daphne
  Globe Amaranth
Impatience, Impatient resolves
  Balsam
Impatient of absence
  Corchorus
Imperfection
  Henbane
Importunity,
Touch me not
  Burdock

Garden Daisy—"I share your sentiments."

Mistletoe—
"I surmount all obstacles.

Balsam—Impatience.

73

Inconstancy
  Evening Primrose
  Wild Ranunculus
Incorruptible
  Cedar of Lebanon
Indecision
  Single China Aster
  Wild Daisy
Independence
  White Oak
  Wild Plum Tree
Indifference
  Candytuft
  Mustard Seed
  Senvy
Indiscretion
  Almond Tree
  Split Reed
Indiscretion,
Docility
  Bullrush
Indolence, Dullness
  Mitraria Coccinea
Industry
  Bee Orchis
  Red Clover
Industry, Domestic virtues,
  Flax
Ingeniousness, Talent
  White Pink
Ingenuity
  Pencil-leaved Geranium
Ingenuous simplicity
  Mouse-eared Chickweed
Ingratitude
  Crowfoot
  Wild Ranunculus
Ingratitude, Childishness
  Buttercup (Kingcup)

Evening Primrose—
Inconstancy.

Wild Plum Tree—
Independence.

White Pink—"You are
fair and fascinating."

Injustice
　Hop
Innocence
　Daisy
　Freesia
Insincerity
　Foxglove
Inspiration, Magic
　Angelica
Instability
　Dahlia
Intellect, Prudence
　Mountain Ash
Intellect, stratagem
　Walnut Tree
Intellectual excellence
　Venice Sumach
Intoxication
　Vine
Invocation
　Water Lily
Jealousy
　French Marigold
　Yellow Rose
Jest, Merriment, Bantering,
　Southernwood
Joy
　Red Dahlia
　Wood Sorrel
Joy, Joys to come
　Lesser Celandine
Joy in sorrow
　Shamrock
Justice
　Rudbeckia
Justice shall be done you
　Sweet-scented Tussilage
Justice shall be done
　Coltsfoot

Hop—Injustice.

Vine—Intoxication.

Red Dahlia—Joy.

75

Keep this for my sake
Veronica Speciosa
Kindness
Marsh Mallow
Kindness and worth
Czar Violet
Knight-errantry
Helmet Flower (Monkshood)
"Lady deign to smile."
Oak-leaved Geranium
Lamentation, Fear
Aspen Tree
Lasting beauty
Stock
Lasting love
Chinese Primrose
Lasting pleasure
Everlasting Pea
Levity, Lightness, Brightness
Larkspur
Let me go
Butterfly Weed
Liberty
Live Oak
Life
Lucerne
Life is sweet
Pyxie
Light-heartedness
Shamrock
Links, Ties
Tendrils of climbing plants
Live for me
Arbor Vitae
Love, Friendship
Arbutus
Love
Myrtle
Red Chrysanthemum
Rose

Oak-leaved Geranium—
"Lady, deign to smile."

Larkspur—Brightness.

Arbutus—
Love or Friendship.

Love at first sight
  Coreopsis Arkansa
  Pyrus Japonica
Love for all seasons
  Furze, Gorse
Love forsaken
  Creeping Willow
Love in idleness
  Wild Violet
Love is dangerous
  Carolina Rose
Love of nature
  Magnolia
Love returned
  Ambrosia
Love's oracle
  Moon Daisy
Love sweet and silent (or secret)
  Honey Flower
Lowliness,
Envy, Remorse
  Bramble
Loyalty
  Shamrock
Luster
  Crowfoot
Luxury
  Horse Chestnut
Magic, Fascination
  Fern
Magnificent beauty
  Calla Aethiopica
Majesty
  First Rose of Summer
Majesty, Dignity
  Imperial Lily
Majesty, Power
  Crown Imperial
Make haste
  Dianthus

Rose (Caroline)—
Love is dangerous.

Honey-flower—
Love sweet and silent.

First Rose of Summer—
Majesty.

77

Malevolence
  Lobelia
Man's footsteps
  White Plantain
Marriage
  Saffron
Maternal affection
  Cinquefoil
Maternal love
  Moss
Maternal tenderness
  Wood Sorrel
Matrimony
  American Linden
Mature charms
  Cattleya
Mature elegance
  Pomegranate Flower
May you be happy!
  Volkamenia
Meanness
  Cuscuta
  Dodder of Thyme
Meditation
  Abutilon
Meditation, Reverie
  Flowering Fern
Meekness
  Birch Tree
Melancholy
  Dark Geranium
  Weeping Willow
  Withered Leaves
Memory
  Syringa
Mental beauty
  Clematis
  Kennedia
Mercy, Zealousness
  Elder

Saffron—Marriage.

Weeping Willow—
Melancholy.

Elder—Mercy.

78

Merriment, bantering, jest
  Southernwood
Message
  Iris
Might
  Night Convolvulus
Mildness
  Mallow
Mirth
  Saffron Crocus
Misanthropy
  Aconite (Wolfsbane)
  Fuller's Thistle (or Teasel)
Modest beauty
  Trillium Pictum
Modest genius
  Creeping Cereus
Modesty
  Lily
  Unique Rose
  White Violet
Mourning
  Cypress
  Weeping Willow
Music
  Bundle of Reeds with their panicles
  Reed
My best days are past
  Colchicum
  Meadow Saffron
My regrets follow you to the grave
  Asphodel
Nature
  Balmia
Neglected beauty
  Throatwort
Never despair
  Watcher by the Wayside
Never-ceasing remembrance
  Everlasting

Saffron Crocus—Mirth.

Rose (Unique)—Modesty.

White Violet—Modesty.

79

Night, Repose
  Convolvulus (Blue, Minor)
Obligation
  Lint
Old age
  Guelder Rose
  Tree of Life
Only deserve my love
  Campion Rose
  Dundee Rambler Rose
Order
  Fir Cone
Ornament
  Daphne
  Hornbeam
Painting
  Auricula
Painting the Lily
  Daphne Odora
Parental affection
  Sorrel
Partake your sentiments
  Double China Aster
Partiality
  Pink Geranium
Participation
  Double Daisy
Passion
  White Dittany of Crete
Paternal error
  Cardamine
Patience
  Dock
  Ox Eye
Patriotism
  American Elm
  Nasturtium
Peace
  Gardenia
  Olive

Auricula—Painting.

Double Daisy—Participation.

Nasturtium—Patriotism.

Pensive beauty
Laburnum
Pensiveness
Cowslip
Perfect loveliness
White Camellia Japonica
Perfection
Pineapple
Perfection of female loveliness
Justicia
Perfidy
Common Laurel in flower
Perplexity
Love in a Mist
Persecution
Checkered Fritillary
Perseverance
Canary Grass
Ground Laurel
Swamp Magnolia
Persuasion
Syrian Mallow
Pertinacity, Rudeness
Clotbur
Philosophy
Pitch Pine
Piquancy, Zest
Lemon
Pity
Pine
Red Camellia Japonica
Platonic Love
Bittersweet
Rose or White Acacia
Play, Sport, Game
Hyacinth
Pleasant recollections
White Periwinkle
Pleasure and pain
Dog Rose

Olive—Peace.

Cowslip—Pensiveness.

White Periwinkle—
Pleasant Recollections.

81

Pleasures of memory
Blue Periwinkle

Poetry
Eglantine (Sweetbriar)

Pomp
Red Salvia

Poor but happy
Vernal Grass

Popular favor
Clatus, Rock Rose

Poverty
Evergreen Clematis

Power
Cress
Crown Imperial
Imperial Montague

Pray for me
White Verbena

Precaution
Goldenrod

Prediction
Prophetic Marigold

Preference
Rose-scented Geranium

Preference,
Fame speaks him great and good
Apple Blossom

Presumption, (also "NO")
Snapdragon

Pretension
Spiked Willow Herb

Pride
Amaryllis
Hundred-leaved Rose
Santenay Rose

Pride of riches
Polyanthus

Privation
Indian Plum (Myrobalan)

Blue Periwinkle—
Pleasures of Memory.

Evergreen Clematis—
Poverty.

Snapdragon—Presumption.

Profit
  Cabbage
Profuseness
  Bindweed
Prohibition
  Privet
Prolific
  Fig Tree
Promptitude, Promptness
  Ten-week Stock
Prosperity, Riches
  Beech Tree
  Corn
  Wheat stalk
Protection
  Bearded Crepis
  Juniper
Provident
  Purple Clover
Prudence,
With me you are safe
  Mountain Ash
Pure and ardent love
  Red Double Pink
Pure and lovely
  Red Rosebud
Pure love
  Single Pink
Purity
  Hyssop
  Corn Flower
  Star of Bethlehem
  White Lily
Purity of heart
  Water Lily
Quarrel
  Broken Corn
Quick sightedness
  Hawkweed

Polyanthus—Pride of Riches.

Bindweed—Profuseness.

Hyssop—Purity.

Rarity
White Ivy
Ready armed
Gladiolus
Reason
Goat's Rue
Recantation
Lotus Leaf
Reciprocal love
Lenten Lily
Reciprocity
Double Chinese Aster
Reconciliation
Filbert
Hazel

Hazel—Reconciliation.

Refinement
Gardenia
White Geranium
Refusal
Striped Carnation
Variegated Pink
Regard
Double Daffodil
Regret
Wisteria
Rejected Addresses
Ice Plant (Ficoides)
Relief
Balm of Gilead
Relieve my anxiety
Christmas Rose
Religious enthusiasm
Schinus
Religious fervor, Belief, Faith
Passion Flower
Religious superstition
Aloe
Remembrance
Pheasant's Eye
Rosemary

Geranium (White)—
Refinement.

Double Daffodil—Regard.

Remorse
  Bramble
  Raspberry
Rendezvous
  Chickweed
Repose, Night
  Blue Convolvulus (Minor)
Reserve
  Maple
Resistance
  Tremella Nestoc
Resolved to win
  Purple Columbine
Restoration
  Persicaria
Retaliation
  Scotch Thistle
Retrospection, Recall
  Silver-leaved Geranium
Return of happiness
  Lily of the Valley
Revenge, Vengeance
  Trefoil
Reverie, Meditation
  Flowering Fern
Reward
  Berry Wreath
Reward of merit
  Bay Wreath
Reward of chastity,
Reward of virtue
  Crown of Roses
Riches, Prosperity
  Beech Treee
  Corn (Maize)
  Wheat Stalk
Rigor
  Lantana
Rivalry
  Rocket

Passion Flower—Belief.

Crown of Roses—
Reward of Chastity.

Wheat—Prosperity.

85

Royalty
Angrec
Rudeness, Pertinacity
Clotbur
Xanthium
Rudeness,
You weary me
Bur
Rupture
Greek Valerian (Blue)
Rupture of a contract
Broken Straw
Rural happiness
Yellow Violet
Rustic beauty
French Honeysuckle
Rustic oracle
Dandelion
Sad memories
Adonis Flos
Sadness, Melancholy
Withered Leaves
Safety
Traveller's Joy
Satire
Prickly Pear
Scandal, Calumny
Hellebore
Sculpture
Hoya (Wax Plant)
Seclusion
Mosses
Secrecy
*Full-blown Rose
placed over two buds
Maidenhair Fern*
Secret love
Yellow Acacia
Self-sacrifice
Andromeda

French Honeysuckle—
Rustic Beauty.

Withered Leaves—
Melancholy.

Virginian Jasmine—
Separation.

Semblance
  Spiked Speedwell
Sensitiveness
  Mimosa (Sensitive Plant)
Sensuality
  Spanish Jasmine
Separation
  Ash-leaved Trumpet Flower
  Carolina or Virginian Jasmine
Serenade, A
  Dew Plant
Severity, Rigor
  Branch of Thorns
Shame, Bashfulness
  Peony
Sharpness of temper
  Barberry
Sickness,
Expectation
  Anemone (Zephyr Flower)
Sickness
  Wood Anemone
Silence, Hush
  Belladonna
Silliness
  Fool's Parsley
Simplicity
  Coxcomb Amaranth
Simplicity, Modesty
  American Sweetbriar
  Single Rose
Sincerity
  Fern
  Garden Chervil
Singularity
  Cockscomb Amaranth
Slander
  Burning Nettle
Sleep
  White Poppy

Wood Anemone—Sickness.

Sweetbriar—Simplicity.

White Poppy—Sleep.

87

Slighted love
  Yellow Chrysanthemum
Snare
  Catchfly
  Dragon Plant
Sociality
  Walnuts
Solace in adversity
  Evergreen Thorn
Solitude
  Heath
  Lichen
Sorcery, Witchcraft
  Enchanters' Nightshade
Sorrow, Sadness
  Purple Hyacinth
  Yew
Sorrowful regret
  Bluebell
Sorrowful remembrance
  Asclepius
Spell, A
  Circaea
  Witch Hazel
Spleen
  Fumitory
Splendid beauty,
Pride
  Amaryllis
Splendor
  Austurtium
  Venice Sumach
Sport, Game, Play
  Hyacinth
Sporting
  Foxtail Grass
Stability, Power
  Cress
Star, A
  Cineraria

Yellow Chrysanthemum.
Slighted Love—

Heath—Solitude.

Purple Hyacinth—Sorrow.

Steadfast piety
Wild Geranium
Stoicism
Box Tree
Stratagem
Walnut
Strength
Cedar
Fennel
Stupidity
Horse-shoe Leaf Geranium
Stupidity, Indiscretion
Common Almond
Submission, Grief
Harebell
Submission, Humility
Grass
Success crown your wishes
Coronella
Succor, Protection
Juniper
Sunbeaming eyes
Scarlet Lychnis
Superior merit
Moss Rose
Surprise
Betony
Truffle
Susceptibility
Wax Plant
Suspicion,
Mushroom (Champignon)
Sweet neglect
Virginian Creeper
Sweetness
White Lily
White Sultan
Sympathy
Balm
Thrift

Cineraria—A Star.

Wild Geranium—
Steadfast Piety.

Walnut—Stratagem.

Talent, Ingeniousness
  White Pink
Tardiness
  Flax-leaved Goldenlocks
Taste
  Scarlet Fuchsia
Tears
  Helenium
Temperance
  Acalia
  Azalea
Temptation
  Apple
  Quince
Thankfulness, Gratitude
  Agrimony
There is no unalloyed good
  Lapageria Rosea
Think of me
  White Clover
Thou art all that is lovely
  Austrian Rose
Thoughts
  Heartsease (Pansy)
Thoughts of absent friends
  Zinnia
Thoughts of heaven
  Snowball (var. Snow Berry)
Thriftiness
  Thyme
Thy frown will kill me
  Currant
Ties, Links
  Tendrils of Climbing Plants
Time
  White Poplar
Timid love
  Maiden Blush Rose
Timidity
  Marvel of Peru

Fuchsia—Taste.

Heartsease—Thoughts.

Thyme—Thriftiness.

Token, A
Laurestina
Touch me not,
Red Balsam
Tranquility
Madwort
Stonecrop
Tranquillize my anxiety
Christmas Rose
Transient beauty
Night-blooming Cereus
Transient impressions
Withered White Rose
Transport of joy
Cape Jasmine
Treachery
Bilberry
Treason
Whortleberry
True friendship
Oak-leaved Geranium
True love
Forget-Me-Not
Truth
Bittersweet Nightshade
White Chrysanthemum
Unanimity
Phlox
Unbelief, Betrayal
Judas Tree
Unceasing remembrance
American Cudweed
Unchangeable, Unfading love
Globe Amaranth
Unchanging friendship
Arbor Vitae
Unconscious beauty
Burgundy Rose
Unconscious sweetness
Lily of the Valley

Christmas Rose—
"Tranquillize my anxiety."

White Chrysanthemum—
Truth.

Rose (White Withered)—
Transient Impressions.

Unconsciousness
Burgundy Rose
Uneasiness
Garden Marigold
Unexpected meeting
Lemon Geranium
Unfading love
Globe Amaranth
Unfortunate attachment or
I have lost all
Mourning Bride
Unfortunate love
Scabious
Union
Lancaster Rose
Whole Straw
Unite against evil, Church unity
Scarlet Verbena
Unity
White and Red Roses together
Unobtrusive loveliness
White Hyacinth
Unpatronized merit
Red Primrose
Unpretending excellence
Red Camellia Japonica
Uprightness, Sentiments of honor
Imbricata
Uselessness
Meadowsweet
Utility
Dried Flax
Grass
Valor, Bravery
Oak Leaves
Variety
China Aster
Rose Mundi
"The variety of your
conversation delights me."
Clarkia

Rose (Burgundy)—
Unconsciousness.

Red Primrose—
Unpatronised Merit.

Grass—Utility.

Vengeance, Revenge
  Trefoil
Vice
  Darnel (Ray grass)
Victory
  Palm
Virtue
  Mint
Virtues, Domestic
  Sage
Vivacity,
Domestic industry
  Houseleek
Volubility
  Abecedary
Voraciousness
  Lupine
Vulgar minds
  African Marigold
War
  Milfoil (Achillea Millefolia)
  York Rose
Warlike trophy
  Indian Cress
Warmth
  Cactus
Warmth of feeling
  Peppermint
Warmth of sentiment
  Spearmint
Warning
  Hand Flower Tree
  Ivy Berry
  Pomegranate Blossom
Watchfulness
  Dame Violet
Weakness
  Moschatel
  Musk Plant
Weeping, Melancholy, Mourning
  Willow

Oak Leaf—Valour.

China-Aster—Variety.

Trefoil—Revenge.

93

Welcome
  Mayflower
Welcome fair stranger
  Wisteria
Welcome me
  Daily Rose
Welcome to a stranger,
Cheerfulness in old age
  American Starwort
Widowhood
  Sweet Scabious
Will you go with me?
  Everlasting Pea
Win me and wear me
  Lady's Slipper
Winning grace
  Cowslip
Winter age, Growing old
  Guelder Rose
Wisdom
  Blue Salvia
  White Mulberry Tree
Wit
  Meadow Lychnis
  Ragged-robin
Wit ill-timed
  Wild Sorrel
Witchcraft, Sorcery
  Enchanters' Nightshade
Witching soul of music
  Oats
With me you are safe
  Ash
  Mountain Ash
Woman's love
  Carnation
Worldliness, Self-seeking
  Clianthus
Worth beyond beauty
  Sweet Alyssum

Rose (Daily)—
"Welcome me."

Guelder Rose—
Growing Old.

Carnation—Woman's Love.

Worth sustained by
judicious and tender affection
  Pink Convolvulus
Worthy all praise,
Strength
  Fennel
You are all that is lovely
  Austrian Rose
You are charming
  Cluster Rose
  Leschenaultia Splendens
You are cold
  Hortensia
You are fair and fascinating
  White Pink
You are hard
  Ebony Tree
You are my divinity
  American Cowslip
You are perfect
  Pineapple
You are the queen of coquettes,
Fashion
  Queen's Rocket
You are radiant with charms
  Ranunculus
You are rich in attractions
  Garden Ranunculus
You are spiteful
  Common Stinging Nettle
You are young and beautiful
  Red Rosebud
You have no claims
  Pasque Flower
You occupy my thoughts
  Purple Violet
You please all
  Branch of Currants
You weary me
  Bur

American Cowslip—
"You are my Divinity."

Pine-apple—Perfection.

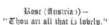

Rose (Austrian) —
"Thou art all that is lovely."

95

You will be my death
  Hemlock
Your charms are engraven
on my heart
  Spindle Tree
Your looks freeze me
  Ficoides (Ice Plant)
Your presence softens my pains
  Milkvetch
Your presence soothes me
  Petunia
Your purity equals
your loveliness
  Orange Blossoms
Your qualities, like your
charms, are unequalled
  Peach
Your qualities surpass your charms
  Mignonette
Your simple elegance charms me
  Diosma
Your whims are quite unbearable
  Monarda Amplexicaulis
Youth
  Primrose
Youthful beauty
  Red Rosebud
  "You are young and beautiful."
Youthful gladness
  Spring Crocus
Youthful innocence
  White Lilac
Youthful love
  Red Catchfly
Zeal
  Arum (Wake Robin)
Zealousness, Mercy
  Elder
Zest, Piquancy
  Lemon

Rosebud (Red) – "You are young and beautiful."

Spring Crocus—Youthful Gladness.

Lemon—Piquancy.